Original title:
Twirling in Tulle

Copyright © 2025 Creative Arts Management OÜ
All rights reserved.

Author: Maxwell Donovan
ISBN HARDBACK: 978-1-80586-019-8
ISBN PAPERBACK: 978-1-80586-491-2

## **Ethereal Threads**

In a world where fluff can float,
Dancing like a silly goat,
With every twist and every spin,
A bouncy laugh from deep within.

Fabrics swirl like candy floss,
In the air, they flip and toss,
An octopus in a tutu's guise,
Tickling noses, oh what a surprise!

Ballet shoes amidst the chaos,
Plies turning flops, with flair embossed,
The audience giggles, can't contain,
As socks go flying, a wild train.

With each grand leap, a snort escapes,
Like gymnasts dressed in funny capes,
Gravity winks, a cheeky tease,
As giggles rise upon the breeze.

**Spirited in Sheen**

In a swirl of glitter and glee,
Dressed like a cupcake, oh me!
With sprinkles of laughter so bold,
Each dance step a story retold.

Bouncing and skipping with flair,
I trip on my dreams unaware.
A giggle escapes from my shoe,
Oh, what a sight—who knew it's true!

### Ethereal Embrace

Whirling like leaves in the breeze,
Caught in a game, oh, if you please!
With arms wide open, I spin around,
Who knew that joy could be this profound?

A lollipop swirl in the sky,
While clouds play peek-a-boo, oh my!
My dress, a rainbow, so bright and keen,
Turning each moment into a scene.

## **Winding Trails of Wonder**

On paths paved with giggles and dreams,
Running with wild, silly schemes.
I twirl with the daisies, share a joke,
My laughter's a melody, never broke.

Through puddles of joy, I leap and bound,
In a world where silliness is found.
With every step, a chuckle escapes,
Oh, what a world, full of shapes!

## A Tapestry of Twirls

In a kaleidoscope of hues,
I dance in patterns, oh, what a muse!
With a shimmy and shake, I take flight,
Gravity's no match when spirits are light.

Cartwheeling through clouds with glee,
The sun winks down, just wait and see!
In this joyful blur, I find my grace,
Each spin a new story I happily chase.

## Fanciful Fantasia

A twirl and a swirl, oh what glee,
Frolicking fairies dance, can't you see?
With frills and froths that float in the air,
Each giggle and wiggle adds lift to their flair.

Ballet shoes squeak on the stage so bright,
In mismatched socks, they don't take flight.
With wispy dimensions that flounce and sway,
They burst into laughter while frogging away.

## The Graceful Unraveling

Scarves in the breeze, a tangled delight,
They trip on their toes in a twisty plight.
With a hop and a skip, they try to untie,
But giggles escape as they tumble and fly.

Each spin a disaster, yet heartily fun,
Chasing after dreams 'til the day is done.
With each crazy caper, a new joke is spun,
In the flurry of laughter, they've already won.

## Dancers in Delicate Dreams

They prance like peas, so round and absurd,
In slippers made out of fluffy old bird.
Each rise and each fall brings a new surprise,
With floppy old hats that cover their eyes.

A pirouette leads to a wobbling stumble,
In riotous circles, with giggles they tumble.
As ribbons entwine, they dance up a storm,
In a whimsical whirl, they create a new norm.

## **Wistful Weavings**

Threads made of sparkles and giggles galore,
With mischief they flutter, then tumble and soar.
Like cotton candy clouds, they bounce in the breeze,
As laughter erupts with the greatest of ease.

Patterns of fun with a twist of the mad,
A wink and a nod, oh how they'd feel glad!
In a world spun of whimsy, they skip and they slide,
Leaving trails of hilarity, filling hearts wide.

## Daring into Dreams

In a world of lace and spins,
A dancer trips, but still she grins,
Her tutu sways, a playful tease,
As laughter dances on the breeze.

With every twirl, she seeks delight,
Her socks mismatched, a comical sight,
She leaps like frogs, and lands like cats,
The audience laughs, oh, how she chats!

Her pirouette bends all the rules,
A goofy leap into the pools,
Of giggles shared and joy unbound,
In tulle and dreams, she's spellbound.

Each step a giggle, each spin a cheer,
This ballet's not for the stoic or drear,
With silly grace, she steals the scene,
In a tutu of laughs, she's the queen.

## Elysian Elegance

A waltz of whimsy, bright and bold,
Dressed like a cupcake, she's uncontrolled,
With frosting hair and shoes that squeak,
She twirls through life, all charm and cheek.

Giggling echoes fill the hall,
As her excitement makes her sprawl,
She glides on air, a jovial sprite,
With fluffy wings, oh, what a sight!

She leaps from there to who knows where,
Her head in clouds, a fluffy hair,
From grace to tripping, she's got it all,
In her whimsical dance, she has a ball.

Amidst the sparkles, laughter reigns,
Her elegance, with silliness, gains,
In a twinkling show, she takes a chance,
With a caper and spin, she leads the dance.

## Cascading Echoes

She fills the air with giggles bright,
As she sways left and leans to the right,
Her dress fluffs out, a cotton cloud,
And everyone watches, joyful and loud.

With cotton candy hanging from her nose,
She twirls around, and around she goes,
Her skips like a rabbit, so nimble and spry,
As she pirouettes, oh my, oh my!

Her feet like springs, they bounce and sway,
With painted cheeks in bright array,
Each spin a giggle, each clap a cheer,
She dances through the crowd, spreading good cheer.

In flowing layers, she glides with grace,
A whirlwind of fun, this humorous chase,
As laughter echoes in rhythm and rhyme,
Her bubbly spirit is truly sublime.

## Enveloping Whispers

In a flurry of lace, she frolics free,
A jester in tulle, as bright as can be,
With mischief in steps and glee in her eye,
She's twinkling today, oh me, oh my!

Her grand plie, a mystical pose,
Sends ripples of laughter where'er she goes,
The music plays tricks on her feet,
As she daintily dances, a joyful beat.

With every predicament, joy overflows,
Her antics unfold like a comic show,
And though she may stumble, she gets up with flair,
Her charisma contagious, spreading everywhere.

With a wink and a giggle, she spins once more,
In this frothy adventure, what wonders in store,
From prancing to spinning, she jests with delight,
In a whirl of laughter, she lights up the night.

## Swaying in Serendipity

A tutu spins with joyful flair,
A swirl of fabric, foe and fare.
The dance of socks, mismatched cheer,
Where laughter trembles, ever near.

A twirl of hair, a skipping beat,
In goofy shoes, we find our feet.
Giggling, sliding down the hall,
Who knew we'd trip, yet never fall?

A cake of frosting on our nose,
While dodging stark and silly woes.
With every slip, we dance and play,
Serendipity leads the way!

## **Cascade of Colors**

A hue of pink and bright canary,
With polka dots, quite legendary.
With every leap, the colors clash,
A rainbow's worth, a vibrant splash.

The purple shoes that squeak with glee,
As we dance wild, yet carefree.
Our outfits clash, a brazen scene,
Like jellybeans in bubblegum sheen.

We spin around, like dizzy birds,
In burst of laughter, joyful words.
Beneath the arch of painted skies,
A cascade forms, to our surprise!

**Floating on Fantasies**

In whimsical dreams of sugar fluff,
We leap and twirl, yet never tough.
A cloud of dessert flies through the air,
As giggles linger everywhere.

We're pirates sailing on a dream,
On a boat of custard and whipped cream.
With every wink and cheeky grin,
We'll battle boredom, sure to win!

A plate of cookies, the anchor drops,
As we navigate, then do the hops.
The fruitcake crew sets sail so fast,
Floating on fantasies, joy amassed!

## The Ballet of Breath

In shoes of squeaks and silly bends,
We flutter like feathers, spastically friends.
With every hiccup, a pirouette near,
The ballet of breath, filled with cheer.

Our laughter wiggles, a flute of joy,
Each step a dance, each spin a ploy.
While sneezes echo through the hall,
We stumble and bumble, yet never fall.

A sneeze and a laugh, a tumble, a roll,
In this ballet, we find our soul.
With every breath, the antics arise,
In this curious dance, joy never dies!

## Fluttering Fantasies

A dress so bright, it spins around,
Like a whirlwind caught on the ground.
With every twirl, it hugs and spins,
Chasing giggles as the fun begins.

Fabrics dance like butterflies,
Creating laughter that never dies.
Little feet prance with glee,
As colors burst, wild and free.

A skip, a hop, then a slide,
Who knew fabric could be a ride?
In this realm of light and fluff,
Every twist simply makes us puff!

So spin and twirl, let humor reign,
For life is short—let's entertain!
With threads that tickle and tickle some more,
Let's dance till our feet can't take it anymore.

## Embrace of Ephemeral Elegance

A swirl of petals in the breeze,
Ticklish fabric that aims to tease.
With every sway, we laugh and play,
Dancing whimsically through the day.

Moments stitch into a quilt,
Of every giggle, joy is built.
Soft textures catch the summer air,
Turning heads as we bounce with flair.

A graceful leap, a cheeky grin,
Watch as it spins, let the fun begin!
Carnival colors light the scene,
Draped in laughter, we feel like queens.

Beneath the sun, we spin with zest,
Life's a joke, so let's jest!
In this playful twirl and flair,
Every moment, love is there.

## Swirls of Softness

Whimsical drapes embrace the day,
Laughing with every colorful play.
A swoosh here, a whoosh there,
It's a grand parade, without a care!

With giggles booming in each spin,
Like a breeze in a world of whim.
From the hem to the top, it's cozy fun,
Making everyone's heart feel young.

Frolic in layers, soft as a cloud,
Humor bright—oh, we feel so proud!
Each little flap sparks a delight,
We'll dance away into the night.

So join the carnival of glee,
In this plush embrace, we are free!
Swirls of softness, laughter to share,
A dress that giggles, beyond compare.

## **A Carousel of Colors**

Round and round in hues so bright,
We laugh and leap, oh what a sight!
With every turn, it whirls and spins,
A party of shades where joy begins.

Painting the air with splashes of fun,
As we dance, the colors run.
Spinning wildly, hearts in flight,
An art show that ignites delight!

From pastels soft to neon bold,
Stories of laughter gracefully told.
Each revolution, a spark of cheer,
Dazzling smiles that draw us near.

Let's whirl away on this merry ride,
In this vibrant world, let's abide!
With colors that tickle and whimsically whirl,
Join the dance, let your spirit unfurl!

**Dance of the Woven Dreams**

In a realm of threads and seams,
Frolic where the laughter beams,
We spin in circles, quite absurd,
With silly steps, we mock the bird.

The fabric flies, oh what a sight,
Giggling as we dance in flight,
A jolly jig, we twist and play,
Finding joy in the light of day.

## The Flutter of Fabrics

Swirling skirts and floppy hats,
We trip like clumsy kittens, chats,
With fabric flapping in the breeze,
We dance and tumble, aim to please.

A sock in hand, a shoe askew,
We leap and frolic, me and you,
The world a stage, we're stars in play,
Laughing as we scamper away.

## Gossamer Reverie

With a whoosh and a swish we glide,
In shimmering layers, we take pride,
Twisted legs and giggles loud,
Beneath our dreamlike, floating shroud.

Ballets gone wrong, a messy art,
Each misstep plays a crucial part,
In this whimsical, wild parade,
Where laughter leads the grand charade.

## The Magic of Movement

A hop, a skip, then a slide,
In our fancy clothes, we confide,
Knotted strings and tangled lace,
A joyful spin, a goofy race.

Our crazy dance, a sight to see,
Bouncing high, so wild and free,
With every twirl, a giggle shared,
In this realm where none are spared.

## Spirals of Splendor

In a dress that spins just so,
I chase my cat, he steals the show.
With each twirl, chaos reigns,
Up ends the rug, spills the grains.

A dip and dash, I hit the ground,
The family dog comes twirling 'round.
He wags his tail, I squeal with glee,
Who knew a dance could bring such spree?

The sofa's now my waltzing partner,
It spins me 'round, oh what a charmer!
With socks as slippers, I glide and slip,
A kitchen floor's my magic trip!

So here I go, a whirlwind spree,
Bumping into mom; she yells, 'Not me!'
In spirals of splendor, laughter's key,
For fun's the dance, come join me free!

## **Ribbons of Radiance**

With ribbons tied and bows a-flare,
I trip and tumble, light as air.
The world around spins bright and bold,
As laughter echoes, pure and gold.

A hat with flair rests on my head,
I join the cat in a dizzy tread.
He jumps and spins without a care,
While I cascade from chair to chair.

The curtains sway as I parade,
I twirl and leap, my plans all laid.
In ribbons bright, they fall like rain,
A joyful mess, no room for pain.

So grab your friend, let's start the game,
In silly dances, we'll find our fame.
With laughter's tune our hearts embrace,
Let's dance through life with joy and grace!

## The Dance of Delirium

In my polka dots, I leap about,
With goofy steps and joyful shout.
The ceiling spins, my socks are slick,
I pirouette, and in I slip.

The pet goldfish gives a knowing glance,
As I attempt a daring dance.
I whirl so fast, I need a seat,
But the sofa calls, 'Oh, take a beat!'

My snacks take flight, popcorn goes high,
As I flail and laugh, oh my, oh my!
In cartwheels of giggles, I find my place,
In this merry madness, pure embrace.

So come and join this jolly spree,
In the dance of delirium, wild and free.
With smiles as bright as the summer sun,
This silly waltz is pure, funny fun!

**Fluttering Hearts**

With fluffy skirts that float and sway,
I prance around just like a play.
My heart is light, my spirit free,
As joy erupts in sunny glee.

A hop and skip, I greet my friend,
We twirl and laugh, the fun won't end.
Just like butterflies, we flit and glide,
In fluttering hearts, we take great pride.

The garden blooms, the flowers cheer,
As we spin and giggle, day is here.
With every leap, the grass gives way,
To our delightful, silly ballet.

So if you've got the mood to dance,
Join me in this fluttering chance.
In hearts that flutter, pure and bright,
Let's chase the giggles, day and night!

## The Elfin Elegy

Little feet that scamper fast,
In a world of fluffs and laughs.
With a wink and a silly jig,
They dance like birds, oh so big!

The hat flies off, oh what a sight,
A spin in circles, pure delight.
Tails of giggles all around,
In the air, they spin and bound!

With pointed ears and mischief clear,
They turn the mundane into cheer.
Jumps and hops, oh what a spree,
Who knew elves could be so free!

At dusk they prance, their shadows leap,
In a game that's lively and deep.
With a plop and a squeal, they gleefully fall,
Their jests and jives, the best of all!

## Echoes of Elation

Round and round, the world does spin,
With giggles shared, where fun begins.
Tiny hands that wave and sway,
Make every moment a festive play!

Jumping jacks and silly songs,
They dance through sunlight all day long.
In skirts that twinkle like the moon,
They swirl about to a joyous tune!

Oh, how they twist, with laughter bright,
With friends beside in sheer delight.
With sparkle shoes and heads held high,
Their rhythm calls, let's touch the sky!

And as the stars begin to peep,
They pirouette, caught in a leap.
With shimmery smiles, they brightly gleam,
In elation's echo, they dream!

## The Graceful Spiral

A twist, a turn, what fun they find,
Frolicking in spirals, two by two, entwined.
With grace unmatched, they reel around,
On tiptoes painted, off the ground!

Every step a comic jest,
With arms that flail, they're at their best.
In a world where laughter leads,
These whirling whiz kids plant their seeds!

Dresses flying, they take the stage,
Filled with antics, all the rage.
Round and round, a sight to behold,
With every giggle, their stories told!

Gliding past like breezy winds,
Their playful hearts, oh how it spins.
Each little whirl a tale of cheer,
In the spiral dance, they disappear!

## Glistening Glimmers

Shimmering friends, with sparkly flair,
In a whimsical frolic, they prance everywhere.
With glimmers bright in the dimmest dark,
They cartwheel past with a joyful spark!

Twirly ribbons wrap round their feet,
As they bounce in harmony to a merry beat.
Silliness flows like a bubbling spring,
While laughter ignites the joy they bring!

Dancing daisies in the lush green,
Each little turn, a crazy scene.
With rosy cheeks and grins so wide,
They bloom like flowers, full of pride!

So here they swirl, a frosted treat,
To the rhythm of fun, they feel complete.
In the glistening dim, so free and bold,
Glimmers of joy, their tales are told!

## Whirls of Whimsy

In a frothy gown, I take my flight,
With each silly step, I feel so light.
Spinning like a jelly on a plate,
Giggles escape, oh, isn't this great?

My friends all stare, slightly bemused,
As I dance with flair, utterly confused.
With a wink and a grin, I take a twirl,
The laughter erupts, what a silly whirl!

With frills that flutter like butterfly wings,
In the chaos of joy, oh, how my heart sings!
A bounce and a bounce, what fun we create,
In this goofy gala, it's never too late.

So here's to the moments of pure delight,
Where tumbling happens from morning till night.
In a puffy cloud, I'll sway and I'll jive,
For in this madness, we truly thrive!

## Gossamer Dreams

In whispers of fabric, I spin so bright,
A ticklish embrace, a textural flight.
With shadows of giggles that dance on the wall,
I leap like a frog, with a giddy sprawl.

Draped like a cupcake, frosting abound,
I bounce through the room, not a care around.
With each playful wiggle, my spirit takes wing,
This funny ballet, oh, what joy it brings!

I trip on a shoelace, and tumble with flair,
In this jolly circus, who needs a chair?
Each moment a treasure, silly and sweet,
In dreams made of laughter, life's quite a treat.

So come join this frolic, let chuckles erupt,
In whimsical layers, we'll dance and disrupt.
With gossamer wishes, the carefree we'll seek,
In this festive whimsy, it's fun that we peak!

## Dance of the Diaphanous

In sheer flowing layers, I leap and I spin,
With jests that unfold, let the frolic begin!
Each twist of my body, a giggle ignites,
As I prance and I bounce under twinkling lights.

Like jelly in sunshine, I shimmer and sway,
With laughter as rhythm, come join in the play.
With a dash and a twirl, I'm a sight to behold,
Chasing the chuckles, both silly and bold.

The air is now filled with whimsical tunes,
As I mingle with friends beneath smiling moons.
In layers of laughter, we twine and we tease,
A lighthearted banquet, an echoing breeze.

So let's spin together, in fervent delight,
With antics and antics that last through the night.
In this dance of the airy, the fun we design,
In a spectacle of joy, may we always shine!

## **Chiffon Reveries**

In gowns of thin whispers, I prance with glee,
Bouncing around like a bee in spree.
With each tiny twist, a new story's born,
A spectacle of laughter, from evening till morn.

I scoot and I zoom, what a sight to chase,
In a flurry of fabric, I find my place.
Spinning in circles, the world in a blur,
With giggles aplenty, oh how we stir!

With friends in this chaos, we waltz with delight,
In the dappled moonlight, everything feels right.
With stumbles and laughter, we find our own beat,
In chiffon reveries, life's journey is sweet.

So let's celebrate joy, twinkling and bright,
In layers of fun, we'll dance through the night.
With whimsical dreams that ignite our hearts' flame,
In this frothy life, this is no silly game!

## **Cloth of Dreams**

In a garden of fabric, I prance with glee,
Fluffy skirts swirling, as light as a bee.
Unruly threads chase my giggles around,
While my feet tap lightly on soft, bouncy ground.

There's a cat who gets jealous, she swats at my hem,
Thinking my dress is a new kind of gem.
Her antics are funny, they make me fall down,
In this whimsical world, I'm the queen of the town.

With every bright twirl, I become quite a sight,
A kaleidoscope whirlwind, a burst of delight.
Friends gather 'round, in their own floppy wear,
We laugh till we tumble, without any care.

But wait, there's a snag in this fabric of fun,
A hook on a branch, and now we all run.
Our laughter a melody, we dance through the hue,
In the land of the silly, where dreams come true.

## Shimmering Strokes of Infinity

Bright ribbons do flutter in the breeze of my spin,
Like creatures of whimsy, where silliness begins.
I prance through the meadow, my dress swirling wide,
Each movement erupts as a giggle inside.

My friends join the revel, adorned like a spree,
With laughter as music, we're wild and carefree.
We twist and we twirl, our imaginations ignite,
Like stars that are laughing through the day and the night.

Oh look at the daisies, they shake with delight,
As I dance past their petals, glowing pure white.
A tumble and roll, we're a circus on grass,
We leap and we bounce, as the moments slip past.

In a painting of joy, each stroke brings a grin,
With textures of laughter that shimmer within.
Round and around, we spin stories of gold,
In this fabric of joy, our adventures unfold.

## A Dance Beneath the Stars

Under the sky, where the moon's light does play,
We twirl like dandelions, merry and gay.
Our feet chase the starlight, two lefts and a right,
In this hilarious waltz, we giggle in flight.

A clumsy old puppy joins in the fun,
Tripping over shadows, yet he's second to none.
He leaps like a dancer, without any care,
Who knew furry pals could be light as air?

With each little turn, and a shimmy here, there,
We spin tales that glitter, like jewels in the air.
The grass, a soft stage, for our frolicsome way,
We laugh with the crickets, till the break of day.

As the world spins around us, a merry-go-round,
That dance under stars makes the night feel profound.
In the laughter of friends, we find our sweet place,
In a comet of joy, we all share the space.

## Spirals of Silk Serenity

In a swirl of bright colors, I gather my crew,
Every spin brings a chuckle, every move feels new.
With sleeves that billow and socks misaligned,
We dance to the rhythm that plays in our mind.

Oh, that little old lady, she stares from her gate,
Her cat seems amused by our silly fate.
We giggle and stumble, as chaos takes hold,
In the fabric of laughter, our stories unfold.

Around and around, like a windmill in flight,
We swirl through the garden, from morning to night.
With petals beneath us, our twinkle toes dance,
In spirals of joy, we give life a chance.

We trip on our dreams, dive into the fun,
With jackets and scarves, our dance has begun.
As echoes of laughter light up the scene,
In this whimsical frenzy, we reign as the queen.

## **Charmed in Cotton Clouds**

A dress made of fluff, a delightful sight,
Spinning 'round corners, what a funny flight.
Feathers in the air, laughter takes its place,
Are those my shoes dancing? Just a little grace.

Puppies chase ribbons, a grand parade,
Slipping and sliding, the silly brigade.
Cotton candy wigs float high with cheer,
Who knew my thoughts could get lost in rear?

Puffs of delight in a whimsical chase,
Twisting and turning, oh, what a race!
Wobbling legs, trying to keep the beat,
Everyone's laughing, can't skip a seat.

Under the sun, we dance so carefree,
Silly visions swirl, just you wait and see.
A tumble, a squeal, we giggle and roll,
Cotton clouds lift spirits, filling the soul.

## Silken Echoes

Waves of soft fabric do tease the air,
Jumping and jiving without a care.
Giggling particles twirl in delight,
Watch out for the puddle, oh, what a sight!

Silk whispers secrets in breezes that play,
Daring all dancers to come out and sway.
A pet cat in motion, with grace so grand,
Turns into a whirlwind, oh man, oh man!

A toss and a twirl, so easy to trip,
Each stumble's a joke, should we take a sip?
Echoes of laughter ring out from afar,
Whirling through colors, we're quite the bizarre.

So come join the fun, let your worries fade,
In the glow of the moon, no fancy parade.
Just heartbeats and laughter, as far as we see,
Floating like feathers, wild and fancy-free.

## Laughter on a Breeze

Fluffy bells chuckle as they sway in the sun,
Bouncing in rhythm, oh, isn't this fun?
Twists and giggles like ripples in time,
Catch the balloons, they're dancing in rhyme.

On a giddy picnic, sandwiches fly,
With flying fruit bowls, let out a sigh.
Socks on the dash, shoes in a heap,
Who put the salad where it should not creep?

The breeze likes to tease as it whispers and plays,
With cookies that run off on adventurous days.
Stumbles and tumbles, all laughter ensues,
In this madcap adventure, you choose your own shoes!

So laugh with the sky, raise your glass for a toast,
To moments of joy we excitedly boast.
With each silly prank, let giggles arise,
As we dance to the music beneath happy skies.

## **Veiled in Glee**

A veil of delight sways, oh what a show,
With balloons afloat, they dance to and fro.
Jumping joyfully in colors so bright,
Splat! There went the cake! Oh, what a sight!

Caught in the breeze, a paper kite flies,
Chasing the giggles and bewildered sighs.
Socks mismatched, and pants a bit tight,
Join hands in the chaos, we're quite a sight!

Pies take a bow, with crusty applause,
As we laugh 'bout the cat, who caused quite the pause.
Sprinkling moments of joy everywhere,
Roaming in circles, with chuckles to spare.

Under the stars, we'll frolic and play,
Trading our stories in hilarious ways.
So here's to the fun and sweet twists we see,
In a world full of laughter, we're ever so free.

## The Fabric of Fantasies

In a closet full of dreams, they play,
Ribbons dancing, leading me astray.
Fabrics whisper laughter in the air,
Mismatched socks, a fashion debonair.

A polka dot cape, a haphazard crown,
Every outfit's a giggle, never a frown.
Spinning like tops, we glide and spin,
Amidst the seams, where the fun begins.

Wearing mismatched shoes, oh what a sight,
Pretending we're stars twinkling at night.
With a twist and a twirl, we stumble and call,
Fashion's a joke; we're having a ball!

The fabric stretches, it pops and flies,
As we leap through the colors, see how it ties.
In the scrapbook of chaos, we play our role,
Crafting a tale from fabric and soul.

## A Whirlwind of Wishes

In a flurry of wishes, we spin and slide,
A cape made of giggles, with nothing to hide.
Fringes of folly, they dance through the day,
We stumble and tumble in the silliest way.

With a swish and a sway, the chaos unfolds,
Forgotten old memories, the funniest molds.
The twinkle of mischief shines bright in our eyes,
As we swirl through the room like a flurry of flies.

Ballet flats squeak, the rhythm is off,
Each misstep brings laughter, a spontaneous scoff.
A hat that's a pickle, a shirt with a cat,
We dance through the rainbow, how silly is that?

We leap like small kangaroos on a spree,
Each twirl is a wonder, it's just you and me.
In a whirlwind of giggles and sparkling cheer,
Here's to the whims that bring joy all year!

## Celestial Choreography

With socks on our hands and hats on our feet,
We march to a tune that's a silly repeat.
Stars in our pockets, we sway and we spin,
Who knew that the cosmos was crafted for grin?

A waltz with a broom, a shimmy with light,
Mapping the galaxies, oh what a sight!
Hopping like comets, we fly through the air,
In this dance of delight, there's magic to share.

Twinkling like fireworks, we burst into laughs,
Crafting our moves with the craziest halves.
Each pirouette bubbles like soda pop bliss,
In this cosmic ballet, it's joy we can't miss.

And though we may trip, we're just rising stars,
We leap over puddles and dance with the cars.
In a universe filled with the odd and the strange,
We're two silly dancers, and we never change!

## Breath of the Ballad

In the breath of a ballad, we glide and we sway,
Singing of silliness in such a fun way.
A sparkly tutu waving like a flag,
With giggles and jiggles, we never lag.

Each purl of the fabric, a tickle of song,
Daring the moments that never feel wrong.
With glittery notes swimming through the air,
Why walk in a line when we can declare?

Hopping like rabbits, unchained by the rules,
Dancing in circles like a bunch of fools.
With a giggle and laugh, we spin like a dream,
In this sweet serenade, we're the best team.

As the music rolls on, we glimmer and gleam,
Each note a reminder to just live the dream.
In the breath of the ballad, we find our own way,
Let's waltz through the chaos and make it our play!

## **Starlit Sashes**

Under the moon, we parade with flair,
Our ribbons flutter, dancing in air.
We trip on toes, a grand charade,
Laughing as we slip, no plans betrayed.

With every spin, a giggle erupts,
We're not ballerinas, just clumsy pups.
A starry night becomes our show,
As wobbly whirlwinds steal the glow.

Confetti crashes, our silly stance,
In tattered skirts, we take a chance.
With glimmers shining, we get more bold,
Sashes swirling, our stories unfold.

So here we are, in our playful dress,
Creating chaos, who would have guessed?
We leap and twirl, a comedic plight,
In the starlit glow, we dance through the night.

## The Art of Ascendance

With every leap, we aim for the sky,
But gravity giggles, oh my oh my!
A graceful rise soon turns into flops,
As we fumble and tumble, we just can't stop.

In fluffy wonders, we lose our way,
A hop, skip, and jump, come join the play.
Our giggles echo, a boisterous sound,
As we spiral up and tumble down.

Balancing beams seem taller today,
Our fancy footwork is here to play.
Flair and laughter are our great friends,
In this mad whirl, the fun never ends.

So raise your skirts and throw back your hair,
Embrace the clumsiness, free as air.
For in this dance, hilarity reigns,
As we laugh ourselves home through life's silly chains.

## Silky Shadows

In the corner of the room, we take our stand,
Shadows pirouette, never quite planned.
An overzealous leap, and down we go,
Silk brushing faces, putting on a show.

Behind the curtains, giggles abound,
As tangled ribbons spin all around.
With every slip, our composure breaks,
Silly dancers with wobbly shakes.

Hats flying high, but only by chance,
As we break into an unplanned dance.
Our silhouettes cast, like playful sprites,
In this chaotic world of comical sights.

So here we twine, in the moon's dim glow,
Silky shadows, putting on a show.
With laughter filling the velvet night,
We embrace our folly, hearts full of light.

## Elegance in Motion

In fancy frocks, we glide and sway,
But elegance fades, come what may.
With every twirl, our balance betrays,
And laughter erupts in the silliest ways.

In the midst of grace, a stumble ensues,
As one leads the charge, wearing mismatched shoes.
The crowd erupts in joyful delight,
Encouraging more of our comical flight.

We're swans in disguise, all ruffled and bright,
Within this ballet, we find pure delight.
With poise, we ascend, then crash with glee,
Our fancy has flair, but we're wild as can be.

So raise a toast to our charming jest,
For elegance is laughter at its very best.
In this crazy dance, we forever will cling,
Amidst all the giggles, we're queens of the fling.

## Veils of Laughter

A frock made of giggles and threads of delight,
Twisting and turning as day turns to night.
With a hop and a skip, off we go,
Chasing our dreams in a comical flow.

There's a twirl and a stumble, oh what a sight,
Laughter erupts like stars burning bright.
Hidden in layers of fabric and fun,
Every spin dances under the sun.

Each bead holds a joke, each seam has a tale,
We laugh 'til our cheeks puff up like the gale.
A pirouette here, a mishap right there,
Life's constant laughter floats up in the air.

When the music plays, we don't have a care,
Floating like feathers, while poking a bear.
So grab your best friend, let's waltz with the wind,
In this silly frolic, where laughter won't end.

## The Spin of Enchantment

Round and round in a whirlwind of cheer,
Giggling at shadows that dance in our sphere.
Each step is a joke, each laugh is a spin,
In the waltz of the whimsies, we joyfully grin.

With ribbons that flutter like butterflies free,
We trip over giggles, just wait and see.
A slip or a twist, we tumble about,
Cackling together, there's never a doubt.

Around we go, like leaves in the gale,
Who knew silly spins could tell such a tale?
With every little stumble, we find something new,
A mishap transformed into humor so true.

In banter and laughter, we twine like the vines,
Every laugh finds a partner, through jests it aligns.
The spins of our stories leave smiles in their tracks,
As we whirl with the whimsy and fortuitous hacks.

**Lace-Laden Reveries**

In layers of lace, where laughter takes flight,
Bouncing on clouds of delights through the night.
A jest here, a giggle, a spin on my toes,
With each little hop, the imagination grows.

We'll dance around corners, in patterns so wild,
Painting the canvas of dreams like a child.
The frills that we flaunt, oh what a delight,
Whispers of laughter, we twinklingly write.

Frolicsome moments, we twirl with the breeze,
At every twinkle, time bends with ease.
Whimsical musings adorned so finely,
Wrapped in the giggles that twine so divinely.

With bursts of joy that weave through the air,
Every spin a new tale, with charm, if we dare.
In laughter, we twirl, with a bounce and a sway,
Creating a tapestry of glee day by day.

## Moonlit Whirls

By the glow of the moon, we shimmy and sway,
Mixing up dreams in a playful ballet.
A hop and a skip, we leap through the night,
In a frolic so playful, our spirits take flight.

The silver beams giggle while twirling us bright,
Waltzing through shadows, we sparkle with light.
A dash of confusion, a sprinkle of glee,
Makes for the best kind of whimsical spree.

As we whirl in a circle, let laughter unfold,
Stories of mishaps and memories retold.
With moonbeams as partners, let's dance and rejoice,
In the fun of the moment, let's give laughter a voice.

With every spin shared, our worries take flight,
In this merry affair, everything feels right.
So let's dance to the rhythm of joy that's unfurled,
In the magical wonder of this twinkling world.

## Hues of Harmony

A pink parade, they swirl around,
Bouncing giggles, fabric sounds.
Chasing laughter, they skip and play,
With twinkling eyes, they seize the day.

In polka dots, the world's a game,
Silly accents, no one's the same.
With every leap, a twist of cheer,
They twirl and spin, without a fear.

The floor is their stage, a dance of glee,
Spinning tales, oh so carefree.
Wings of joy in every spin,
In colorful bliss, where fun begins.

Like butterflies caught in a breeze,
Their giggles float with such sweet ease.
In hues so bright, it's hard to tell,
If they're laughing, or casting a spell.

## Whispers of Wind and Fabric

In the garden where daisies bloom,
Socks mismatched, a funny costume.
With capes of cloth, they chase the sun,
As breezes tug—it's all in fun!

A flurry of limbs in colors bold,
Their joy spread wide, a sight to behold.
Whispers rustle, a silent cheer,
A raucous dance where fun draws near.

With silly hats adrift in the air,
They spin and flourish without a care.
Each twirl's a note in a playful song,
In this fabric ballet, nothing's wrong!

As laughter swirls like autumn leaves,
They frolic here, where mischief weaves.
A patchwork quilt of giggle and sigh,
In whispers soft, let the spirits fly.

## The Graceful Spin

With ribbons bright, like rainbows wide,
They take a leap, no need to hide.
A waltz of whimsy, they flip and sway,
Graceful giggles in bright display.

Round and round, like a dizzy bee,
Silk and laughter, what a spree!
Their gentle spins, a playful art,
Each frolic captured, a joyful heart.

In playful tussles, they dance anew,
With every step, a laugh breaks through.
So round they go, in fits of glee,
A merry dance, just wait and see!

In this merry-go round, together they leap,
Chasing giggles that never sleep.
The rhythm of joy, a fun-filled fling,
In the sway of the fabric, let laughter ring!

## **Fluttering Through Fantasia**

Fluffy clouds and endless dreams,
Frolicking where the sunlight beams.
In a splash of colors, they shout hooray,
Dancing along the merry way.

Caught in a giggle, they spin and glide,
With glittering eyes, they choose to abide.
Every leap brings smiles and delight,
Their whimsical charms a joyful sight.

With swathes of joy, their laughter swells,
In a circus of giggles, no need for bells.
Each flap and flourish a cheeky tease,
In this playful dance, their hearts find ease.

Through cascades of fabric, they leap and soar,
In a world of fun, who could ask for more?
Reveling in dreams, they twirl and spin,
A festival of joy, where all begin.

## Enigma of the Fairy's Skirt

A creature flits with laughter bright,
Ruffles spin in the morning light.
She twirls and spins, a playful tease,
Oh my, her dance could start a breeze!

Beneath her wings, the secrets play,
A waltz of whimsy, night and day.
With tiny shoes and a cheeky grin,
Her charm is what draws us all in!

In every twist, a giggle hides,
As she jumps, the fun abides.
A whirlwind of joy, a giddy spree,
What a sight, oh can't you see?

As shadows stretch and laughter flows,
Her frolics bring out hidden prose.
With each petite pirouette, a thrill,
Oh, what a sight, we love her still!

## **Diaphanous Dances**

Veils of whispers skim the floor,
Each step a giggle, who could ignore?
A jester's leap, a clownish slip,
The graceful drop of a lopsided flip!

Chiffon clouds bounce and sway,
Follow the laughter, don't delay!
With every glide, a scene unfolds,
A dainty story, oh how bold!

The fabric flows like silly streams,
We're caught up in our wildest dreams.
In slanted spins, and silly sweeps,
She twirls and twirls while mischief leaps!

Each layer lighter, witty and air,
She teases gales with flair and dare.
What a ruckus, what a sight,
Her dance, the bliss of pure delight!

**Swaying in Serenity**

A gentle breeze starts to sway,
As giggles chase the gloom away.
In rhythmic runs, the spirits rise,
With flapping skirts and cheerful sighs!

On dainty toes, she takes a chance,
Around the room, a silly dance.
With swirls of charm and blissful cheer,
She twirls to beckon those who near!

A soft sashay, a playful spin,
Enticing joy from deep within.
What fun, what frolic, what delight,
In this dance of giggles, bright!

As day fades to a starry night,
Her whimsy shines, a joyful light.
With laughter echoing in the breeze,
She sways and spins with perfect ease!

## **Threads of a Celestial Sonata**

In moonlit rays, she stamps her feet,
An orchestra of giggles, oh so sweet.
With each strand woven in delight,
She dances under stars so bright!

A ruffled edge, a sparkling wink,
Her playful ways make shadows blink.
Her swing and sway, a gleeful plot,
In cosmic threads, she dances, caught!

The night, it hums a merry song,
Join the fun, come dance along!
With every twirl, a spark ignites,
A jolly tale that feels just right!

As gales of laughter fill the skies,
Her whimsical heart, it never lies.
With breezy spins and joyous sound,
In every note, pure glee is found!

## Momentary Magic in Motion

In a swirl of fluff and giggles,
Tiny feet leap, the world jigs.
With every spin, a puff of joy,
Unruly waltz of a bounce-toy.

Laughter bounces off the walls,
As cotton clouds rise in stalls.
A comical flip, a twist, a twirl,
Silly smiles in every whirl.

Chasing shadows, light and free,
Turning life to jubilee.
With every hop, watch spirits rise,
Whimsical leaps beneath the skies.

In this moment, time's a blur,
Watch them dance, no need for spur.
Caught in rhythms, pure delight,
Just a jolly, fleeting sight.

## **Whirling Wonderment**

Round and round, the fun begins,
With socks that slip, and cheeky grins.
The frosted tulle lifts high in air,
Unruly ballet, beyond compare.

Every bounce makes laughter bloom,
Miniature pirouettes in the room.
A parade of giggles, what a scene,
With dandelion dreams, and mischief unseen.

They spin like tops upon the floor,
A clumsy dance, who could ask for more?
Fluffy chaos in playful haze,
Filling this space with silly displays.

From one corner to the next,
A joyous mess, no need for text.
In this quirky, jovial dance,
Life feels like a fun-filled chance.

## Whispers of Gossamer

Gentle whispers float all around,
In a world of whimsy, lost and found.
Little giggles with every sway,
As they float on gossamer ballet.

Fluffy skirts and wobbly feet,
Every stomp is a magical feat.
Like butterflies chasing after the sun,
In this silly dance, everyone's won.

In the flurry, joy is found,
Spinning yarns of laughter abound.
With every glance, the silliness grows,
As petals of mirth scatter like prose.

Cotton candy clouds in playful mix,
In each little step, a new bag of tricks.
Watch them flitter, a tug on a friend,
With whimsy like this, who needs to pretend?

## Dance of the Dreamcatcher

A circle of joy, like dreamers play,
Their giggles float like clouds in May.
Lopsided leaps, wild and spry,
Captured laughter that dances high.

With every twirl, mischief ignites,
A dreamcatcher spun in the moonlight.
Petals of laughter in the air,
In this cavalcade, all hearts flare.

Frilly adornments, sways to a beat,
Racing giggles become a treat.
Spinning stories, they flit and fly,
Boundless cheer beneath the sky.

In their frolic, nothing is wrong,
Each silly move feels like a song.
Together they dance, a charming surprise,
In a world where playfulness never dies.

## **Ethereal Embrace**

In a swirl of fabric, I take my chance,
Tripping on air in a flowing dance.
With every twirl, giggles erupt,
As I leap like a bird, quite abrupt.

A cascade of ruffles surrounds my feet,
I step on my hem, oh what a feat!
The mirror laughs back, a comical sight,
As I pirouette under the soft twilight.

Laughter pours forth, a joyous sound,
Clumsy ballet in skirts all around.
With each little spin, I create a storm,
In this playful frolic, I feel so warm.

Caught in a jig, the fun's at its peak,
My artistic flair—unique but cheek.
Roll with the laughter, with grace and delight,
In a fabric-filled frenzy, I twirl into night!

## Lace and Laughter

A skirt of lace spins circles of fun,
I feel like a star, but it's all a pun.
My feet are tangled, but spirits are high,
As I chase after dreams, oh my oh my!

With each little twist, a giggle slips free,
Whirling and swirling, oh look at me!
Caught in this dance, with ribbons I'll play,
Turning mishaps into a grand cabaret.

Beneath the lights, the humor ignites,
A soft patch of laughter, the best of sights.
In a waltz of mischief, my heart takes flight,
Who knew that soft lace could be such a delight?

With every step, I balance and sway,
Unraveled and tumbled, I dance away.
In the froth of the moment, I find my bliss,
In a haze of giggles, there's nothing I miss!

## Moonlit Pirouettes

Under the moonlight, I make a stance,
A dress that sparkles, a chance to prance.
With arms wide open, I spin with glee,
Laughing so hard, I can hardly see.

Around and around, I whirl like a breeze,
Tripping on shadows, oh, how they tease!
With every misstep, the chuckles grow loud,
As I trip o'er starlight, feeling quite proud.

The night sky winks, a conspirator's game,
My dance is a riot, no two steps the same.
In a moonlit ballet of whimsy and cheer,
I laugh at my folly, its charm drawing near.

A tapestry spins, full of giggles and flair,
Underneath the stars, I dance without care.
With twinkling delight, I frolic and slide,
In this silly soirée, there's nowhere to hide!

## Fantasia in Folds

In folds of laughter, I take my leap,
Adventurous dreams that tickle and creep.
With a flap and a flutter, I'm lost in the fold,
Making memories brighter than diamonds or gold.

A whirl of exuberance, watch me go round,
With every mischief, new giggles are found.
Like a wild wind, I dance through the night,
Woven in joy, what a comical sight!

As I twizzle and twist, the chaos unfolds,
My skirt dances wildly, with secrets it holds.
In this surreal world, I have found my place,
Wrapped in a frolic, I savor the pace.

So here I remain, with laughter so bold,
In my whimsical world, no stories left untold.
In the fabric of dream, I find my parade,
In a playful escapade, I am unafraid!

## Airborne Whimsy

A feathered hat flies past my nose,
With giggles hidden where the breeze flows.
A cat in a tutu strikes a pose,
While squirrels dance on tiptoes in rows.

Balancing books atop my head,
I twirl like I'm a dandelion spread.
Laughter echoes, the world's a thread,
In this carnival of joy, I'm fed.

Trees wink with their leafy surprise,
As butterflies wear fancy ties.
I kick up the leaves, my spirit flies,
In this silly land where fun never dies.

So join the parade, don't be shy,
We'll spin and swirl, my oh my!
With every bounce, a friendly goodbye,
In a world so bright, we just can't lie.

## **Poised in Petals**

In a garden where silliness blooms,
The flowers giggle in colorful costumes.
Daisies wear hats, and roses swoon,
While bumblebees dance to a playful tune.

A plump little bunny hops with flair,
Wearing a jacket made of air.
He twitches his nose, no time to spare,
In this petal party, we have laughter to share.

With vines that swing like a wild ballet,
And fireflies winking at the end of the day.
We step in puddles; oh, what a play!
As the sun dips low and shadows sway.

So grab a daffodil, take a chance,
Let's join this whimsical flower dance.
In the silly moments, our hearts enhance,
With petals and giggles, we do our prance.

## The Mysterious Flare

A hat appeared from who knows where,
With a twinkle that danced in the air.
It grinned so wide, an odd affair,
As it led us to who-knows-where.

The moon wore socks and a spotted tie,
While raccoons conducted with a pie in the sky.
Strange tales waft in the breeze nearby,
Tickling our thoughts; oh, what a high!

Swirls of laughter leak from doors,
Past the windows, where silliness soars.
Each knock stirs magic from tiled floors,
As the night spills secrets, our hearts want more.

The flare hums softly, a tune so rare,
With joy and mischief hanging in the air.
We dance with shadows, feel the flair,
In this mysterious world, there's nothing to compare.

**Floating Through Daydreams**

On a cloud of marshmallows, we skate,
With gummy bears dancing to the fate.
Ducking under chocolate waterfalls,
We giggle and twirl, as fun enthralls.

Giraffes wear spectacles, reading in style,
Unicorns prance with a glittery smile.
Lost in daydreams, let's linger awhile,
As we play hopscotch with stars in a pile.

The sun beams down, a golden glow,
As we leap through puddles of rainbow flow.
In this cartoon realm, come join the show,
Where laughter is counting, and joy starts to grow.

So grab a friend and float along,
In the bouncy world of giggles and song.
With each silly moment, we belong,
In the tapestry of dreams, we are strong.

## Stitches of Stardust

In a dress of fairy dreams, I prance,
Adorned with sparkles, ready to dance.
My cat's the judge, in collar so bright,
Critiquing my moves under the moonlight.

Each spin unravels a thread or two,
The fabric giggles, as if it knew.
I step on toes of my absent cat,
He just rolls over, that's where he's at.

With every twirl, my snack flies away,
A trail of crumbs from yesterday's play.
I chase a chipmunk, oh what a sight,
Imagining fables, on this silly night.

Stitches of stardust, in knots I entrap,
Whirling and twirling, no time for a nap.
My friends in the backyard join the hullabaloo,
We laugh at the stars, and our silly view.

## The Loop of Luft

In the garden, we frolic, in circles we fly,
A loop of air, as clouds drift by.
With each graceful leap, I twirl and I shout,
My wig takes a flight, oh what a clout!

A grasshopper giggles as I lose my grip,
My hat sails above in a whimsical trip.
The neighbors all chuckle, eyes big as the moon,
While I chase my attire, they croon a fun tune.

Luft in my curls, in spirals it sways,
Laughing with flowers on bright sunny days.
I pilot my laughter, I soar and I sway,
In a loop of delight, come join if you may!

The world spins around, and I join in the act,
My sock puppet dog, he always reacts.
With every grand leap, the fun never halts,
In this joyful ballet, no reason to vault!

## The Lightness of Being

A jump in the air, like a butterfly's flight,
Floating on clouds, oh what a delight!
With wiggles and jiggles, I skip and I twine,
In this realm of giggles, the place is divine.

Up on my toes, and off with my cape,
Pretending I'm bold, a hilarious shape.
The squirrels join in, a flamboyant parade,
While I dance clumsily, trying to invade.

The neighbors peek out, oh dear what a sight,
They see me flailing, under the moonlight.
But laughter erupts, it echoes so keen,
For the lightness of being is truly a scene.

In this carnival atmosphere, full of cheer,
I swirl like confetti, without any fear.
So here's to the chuckles, let's make this our song,
Dancing with shadows, where we all belong!

## Spirited Swirls

With ribbons and sparkles, I leap and I glide,
Spirited swirls take me on a fun ride.
Around the old oak, I spin on one foot,
Trying to catch squirrels, oh that would be cute!

The dog watches closely, with eyes full of glee,
As I trot and I swirl like a kite in the breeze.
My beret goes flying, oh where did it land?
A funny old dance, that no one had planned.

The wind starts to chuckle, it tickles my nose,
With every round cheer, my giggle just grows.
I bump into daisies, they rustle and sigh,
In this festival whirl, we reach for the sky.

So twirl with me freely, with laughter in tow,
We'll spin our own stories, allowing joy to flow.
In the land of ridiculousness, we'll find our refrain,
With each spirited swirl, let's dance in the rain!

**Elegance in Motion**

She danced like a cake on a table,
Her dress fluffed up, ready and able.
With each joyful leap, a sly grin,
Who needs a crown when you fly with a spin?

The party hats sat with envy and glares,
As she twirled 'round, knocking over some chairs.
A caper of laughter, she couldn't resist,
In a swirl of delight, she truly existed.

Guests giggled softly, clutching their sides,
Watching her glide like a duck on the tides.
With every faux pas, more fun did abide,
In her gown of pure joy, she was full of pride.

Her shoes tapped the rhythm of joy in perfect sync,
A cacophony loud, it made them all think,
Maybe elegance lives in each funny fall,
And the dance of delight truly welcomes us all.

## A Spin of Silken Starlight

She whirled like a dervish with sparkly shoes,
Gathering giggles and light-hearted snooze.
With her cape fluttering, she's dizzy, it's true,
Yet the stars in her eyes keep the laughter anew.

In the corner, they had popcorn to munch,
As she spun by repeatedly, a thrilling punch.
"A comet!" they shouted, "Oh what a sight!"
Her cape flowing back, a heavenly flight.

Just like a squirrel with a fondness for nuts,
She twinkled and jumped, while they laughed like a bunch.
Who knew silken starlight could drip from the sky,
When you dance with your heart and leave worries to fly?

With her head in the clouds and feet in a whirl,
She gave all their frowns a fantastic twirl.
For laughter and joy are the best kind of night,
Underneath all her spins, there's pure starlit delight.

## Petals in the Breeze

She danced like a leaf caught in play,
Spinning round when she lost her way.
With a swirl and a leap, she would dart,
Petals of giggles were tossed from her heart.

A garden of friends tossed their cares in the air,
Chasing her laughter, a carefree affair.
Dandelions twinkled, so playful and free,
They swayed to her rhythm, like leaves on a spree.

With grace (or perhaps lack thereof) in her stride,
Her antics ignited a jubilant ride.
The daisies all chuckled, joined in with glee,
What a bouquet of joy that blossomed to be!

As the sun dipped low and shadows grew long,
They twirled 'round together, a laugh-filled throng.
In the light of the moon, they spun out their dreams,
Each petal of laughter burst forth in bursts of beams.

## **Veils of Vivid Imaginations**

In a world of her dreams, she concocted a plan,
To dance like a jelly, as kooky as can.
With veils trailing behind, she twirled with delight,
Her mind full of fanciful, whimsical flight.

With adventures and critters all sprouting in cheer,
The crowd looked perplexed, but they loved her, oh dear!
She held on to giggles, they hung on her hem,
Each spin was a giggle, a whimsical gem.

She flopped like a gopher, she twisted and spun,
Creating a whirlwind of laughter and fun.
They tried to keep up, but alas, they would slip,
With dreams stitched in fabric, this dance was a trip.

As the music echoed and joy filled the air,
Her veils danced brightly with dreams everywhere.
In this wild merry ballet, all worries took flight,
With vivid imaginations, they spun through the night.

## **Veiled Joy**

A hat with a twist, so grand and bright,
Balancing well on my head, what a sight!
With each little step, I trip and I spin,
Giggles erupt as I tumble, oh win!

The world is a stage, I'm the star of clowns,
In frills and in fluffs, I dance upside-downs.
Friends join my frolic, all laughter and cheer,
With hats flying high, we've conquered all fear!

## Enchanted Whirl

In a forest of laughter, we stumble and glide,
In costumes that sparkle, our joy cannot hide.
A twirl of bright colors, a slip on the grass,
With giggles and smiles, let the moments pass.

The squirrel joins in, with a cap and a bow,
We dance round in circles, let the wind blow!
With just one small trip, oh what can go wrong?
Our jig is a laughter, we're singing our song!

## Dance of the Soft Shadows

Beneath the bright moon, we twinkle and shake,
Pretending to fly, oh, what joy we make!
A shuffle, a spin, we're lost in the night,
With shadows that giggle, what a whimsical sight!

In puddles we splash, like stars that fell down,
With laughter and glee, we mirror our crown.
As light turns to dark, we veil our delight,
In a game of disguise, we dance till first light.

## Delicate Spirals

In ribbons and bows, we tumble around,
With silly old hats, our giggles resound.
Each step is a doodle, a splash of pure fun,
We whirl like dervishes, unable to run!

The breeze starts to tickle, we wobble and sway,
With friends in the mix, the world's turned to play.
A spin gives a stumble, we all fall with grace,
Kindred spirits adrift in a whimsical race!

## Balancing Bliss

A bird on a wire, a wig on a head,
Juggling too much, but still in my bed.
My socks match my shirt, or so I believe,
The laughter erupts, there's joy to achieve.

With one foot in front, and the other behind,
I dance like a noodle, all tangled, you'll find.
The cat steals my seat, as I trip over dreams,
Life's full of giggles and wild, silly schemes.

Spinning like tops with no end in sight,
I slide on the floor, all wrong feels so right.
The cake on my face is a badge of my fun,
Who knew being clumsy could become such a run?

With friends all around, the chaos is grand,
We'll tip over tables just to make a stand.
In the land of the silly, we bounce to the beat,
Embracing the whimsy, we feel so complete.

## Dancing with the Light

Glimmers and glances, the sun's little rays,
  I stomp on the floor, in a dainty ballet.
Like shadows at dusk, I lose my own way,
But hey, what's the rush? It's just a fun play.

Spinning like fireflies caught in a jar,
I trip over laughter, it leads me so far.
In polka-dot skirts, we shimmer and sway,
A dance party waiting, come join in the fray!

Bouncing around like a puppy untamed,
Each giggle and grin is a victory claimed.
I twirl 'round the room, like a muffin's delight,
What joy can we find in this beautiful light?

So let's paint the walls with a splash of our grace,
A leap and a whirl in this silly rat race.
With each twinkling moment, our spirits take flight,
Together we laugh in the glow of the night.

## A Chorus of Colors

When colors collide in a beautiful mess,
I wear polka dots, my own fashion press.
Dressed as a taco, I prance down the lane,
Laughing with rainbows, we sway through the pain.

A jellybean hat in a world full of grey,
I whirl like a dervish, come join in the play.
The flowers are giggling, the sun's in on it,
With each silly step, we all seem to fit.

Splatters of pink from a pie on my face,
Who knew that chaos could be such a grace?
In this joyful parade of eccentricities bright,
We're dancing together into the night.

With capes made of laughter, we're heroes today,
Exploring this wonder with nothing to weigh.
Each color a note in this anthem so sweet,
A chorus of giggles, we can't be beat!

## Threads of the Heart

With ribbons and strings, a tapestry spun,
I weave in the laughter; oh, isn't this fun?
The cat in my lap is my woven delight,
As the fabric of friendship wraps us up tight.

In stitches of humor, we craft our own fate,
With each cheeky joke, we can't help but relate.
A patchwork of memories, pieced together fast,
Each chuckle a thread, our joy unsurpassed.

With yarn in my hand, I knit up a show,
Where silliness reigns, and the giggles overflow.
From knots of the past, we giggle and chime,
Every twist of the loom a rhythm in rhyme.

So join in the weaving, the fun never parts,
Creating a story, a dance of our hearts.
In this cozy circle, our positions secure,
With laughter's warm blanket, we're silly and pure.

www.ingramcontent.com/pod-product-compliance
Lightning Source LLC
Chambersburg PA
CBHW060123230426
43661CB00003B/314